YOUR MAGICAL
Manifestation
JOURNAL

A guided journal to start each day
feeling calm and energized

DR. AMRITA KUMARI

BLUEROSE PUBLISHERS
India | U.K.

Copyright © Dr. Amrita Kumari 2024

All rights reserved by author. No part of this publication may be reproduced, stored in a retrieval system or transmitted in any form or by any means, electronic, mechanical, photocopying, recording or otherwise, without the prior permission of the author. Although every precaution has been taken to verify the accuracy of the information contained herein, the publisher assume no responsibility for any errors or omissions. No liability is assumed for damages that may result from the use of information contained within.

BlueRose Publishers takes no responsibility for any damages, losses, or liabilities that may arise from the use or misuse of the information, products, or services provided in this publication.

For permissions requests or inquiries regarding this publication, please contact:

BLUEROSE PUBLISHERS
www.BlueRoseONE.com
info@bluerosepublishers.com
+91 8882 898 898
+4407342408967

ISBN: 978-93-5989-262-7

Cover design: Daksh
Typesetting: Tanya Raj Upadhyay

First Edition: January 2025

Welcome Letter to the awesome person

Name-_____

Details- _____

Phone No- _____

Profession- _____

INTENTION for buying this journal or purpose of journaling.

Hello beautiful souls,

I congratulate you for taking one beautiful step towards your self-transformation. I can say this because not me but many have transformed their lives with beautiful practice of journaling.

- When you write, your subconscious mind along with your mind and soul is working as one unit and help you remove mind blocks and achieve what you want to achieve.

- Any thing which is on paper has more probability to be true according to law of attraction so,

    I welcome you to this awesome journey.

    Lots of abundance and more power to you.

Dr. Amrita Kumari
Your Life Coach Healer and Planner

Rules to Follow

- ✓ *Be kind to yourself*
- ✓ *Do not quit or do not blame yourself or others if you are not consistent.*
- ✓ *If you miss one day, start from next day.*
- ✓ *Carry this journal everywhere, every day.*
- ✓ *Focus only on 1 percent progress every day.*
- ✓ *Everything is perfect the way it is.*

GRADING - (0 – 10)	
Health	
Career	
Love	
Spirituality	
Family	
Friends	
Fun	
Money	

WHEEL OF LIFE

WHERE I AM

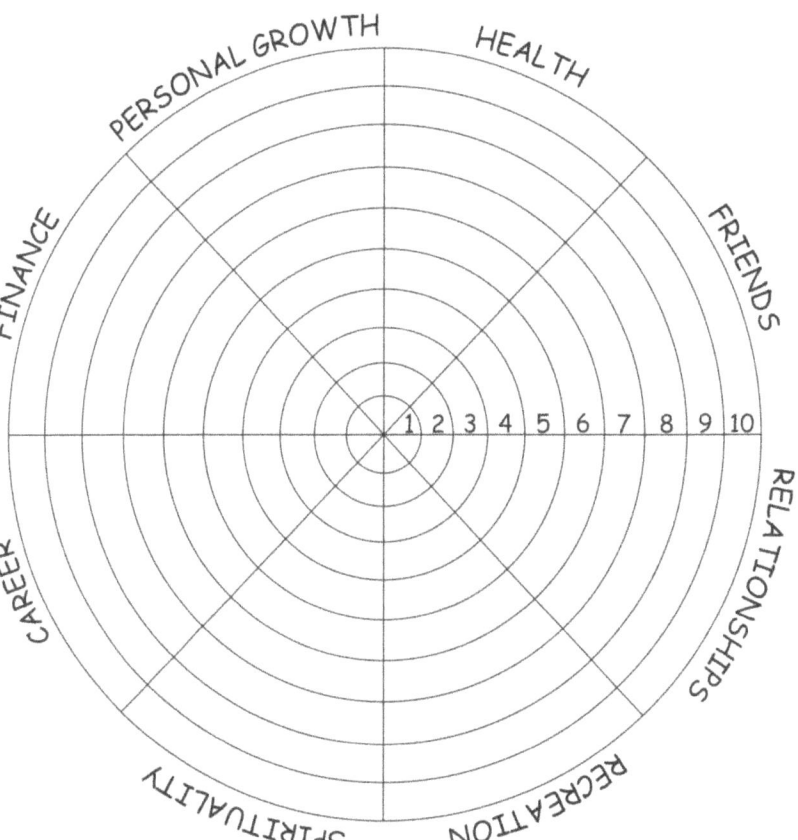

KICK START THE DAY

Morning Routine

S - Silence - 2min

A - Affirmation - 2 min

V - Visualisation - 10 min

E - Exercise - 30 min

R - Reading - 5 to 10 min

S - Scribing - Thank you letter to universe or gratitude letter.

We follow this every morning.

MORNING HABITS

Day-1

Silence + Meditation

_____
_____
_____
_____
_____

Journaling Gratitude

_____
_____
_____
_____
_____

INTENTION of day

_____
_____
_____
_____
_____

MORNING HABITS

Day-2

Silence + Meditation

_____
_____
_____
_____
_____

Journaling Gratitude

_____
_____
_____
_____

INTENTION of day

_____
_____
_____
_____
_____

MORNING HABITS

Day-3

Silence + Meditation

___

Journaling Gratitude

___

INTENTION of day

___

MORNING HABITS

Day-4

Silence + Meditation

_____
_____
_____
_____
_____

Journaling Gratitude

_____
_____
_____
_____
_____

INTENTION of day

_____
_____
_____
_____
_____

MORNING HABITS

Day-5

Silence + Meditation

_____
_____
_____
_____
_____

Journaling Gratitude

_____
_____
_____
_____

INTENTION of day

_____
_____
_____
_____
_____

MORNING HABITS

Day-6

Silence + Meditation

_____
_____
_____
_____
_____

Journaling Gratitude

_____
_____
_____
_____
_____

INTENTION of day

_____
_____
_____
_____
_____

MORNING HABITS

Day-7

Silence + Meditation

_____
_____
_____
_____
_____

Journaling Gratitude

_____
_____
_____
_____
_____

INTENTION of day

_____
_____
_____
_____
_____

ACTION MODE

DAY-1

Daily Journaling (morning)

Gratitude Letter

Habit 1-

Drink Water-   (Hot Water *with* Lemon)

(Hot Water with cumin & saunf)

Exercise-   Yes/No

Duration-

Feeling After Exercise-

Works to be done today-   Done/Not done

Work 1

Work 2

Work 3

Work 4

Work 5

Night Routine

How was your Day-

What are the things you achieved

What you are thankful of-

ACTION MODE

DAY-2

Daily Journaling (morning)

Gratitude Letter

Habit 1-

Drink Water-   (Hot Water *with* Lemon)

              (Hot Water with cumin & saunf)

Exercise-   Yes/No

Duration-

Feeling After Exercise-

Works to be done today-   Done/Not done

Work 1

Work 2

Work 3

Work 4

Work 5

Night Routine

How was your Day-

What are the things you achieved

What you are thankful of-

ACTION MODE

DAY-3

Daily Journaling (morning)

Gratitude Letter

Habit 1-

Drink Water- (Hot Water *with* Lemon)

(Hot Water with cumin & saunf)

Exercise- Yes/No

Duration-

Feeling After Exercise-

Works to be done today- Done/Not done

Work 1

Work 2

Work 3

Work 4

Work 5

Night Routine

How was your Day-

What are the things you achieved

What you are thankful of-

ACTION MODE

DAY-4

Daily Journaling (morning)

Gratitude Letter

Habit 1-

Drink Water-   (Hot Water *with* Lemon)

                 (Hot Water with cumin & saunf)

Exercise-   Yes/No

Duration-

Feeling After Exercise-

Works to be done today-   Done/Not done

Work 1

Work 2

Work 3

Work 4

Work 5

Night Routine

How was your Day-

What are the things you achieved

What you are thankful of-

ACTION MODE

DAY-5

Daily Journaling (morning)

Gratitude Letter

Habit 1-

Drink Water-   (Hot Water *with* Lemon)

                      (Hot Water with cumin & saunf)

Exercise-   Yes/No

Duration-

Feeling After Exercise-

Works to be done today-   Done/Not done

Work 1

Work 2

Work 3

Work 4

Work 5

Night Routine

How was your Day-

What are the things you achieved

What you are thankful of-

ACTION MODE

DAY-6

Daily Journaling (morning)

Gratitude Letter

Habit 1-

Drink Water-   (Hot Water *with* Lemon)

                    (Hot Water with cumin & saunf)

Exercise-   Yes/No

Duration-

Feeling After Exercise-

Works to be done today-   Done/Not done

Work 1

Work 2

Work 3

Work 4

Work 5

Night Routine

How was your Day-

What are the things you achieved

What you are thankful of-

ACTION MODE

DAY-7

Daily Journaling (morning)

Gratitude Letter

Habit 1-

Drink Water-   (Hot Water *with* Lemon)

                 (Hot Water with cumin & saunf)

Exercise-   Yes/No

Duration-

Feeling After Exercise-

Works to be done today-   Done/Not done

Work 1

Work 2

Work 3

Work 4

Work 5

Night Routine

How was your Day-

What are the things you achieved

What you are thankful of-

ACTION MODE

DAY-8

Daily Journaling (morning)

Gratitude Letter

Habit 1-

Drink Water-   (Hot Water *with* Lemon)

              (Hot Water with cumin & saunf)

Exercise-   Yes/No

Duration-

Feeling After Exercise-

Works to be done today-   Done/Not done

Work 1

Work 2

Work 3

Work 4

Work 5

Night Routine

How was your Day-

What are the things you achieved

What you are thankful of-

ACTION MODE

DAY-9

Daily Journaling (morning)

Gratitude Letter

Habit 1-

Drink Water-   (Hot Water *with* Lemon)

(Hot Water with cumin & saunf)

Exercise-   Yes/No

Duration-

Feeling After Exercise-

Works to be done today-   Done/Not done

Work 1

Work 2

Work 3

Work 4

Work 5

Night Routine

How was your Day-

What are the things you achieved

What you are thankful of-

ACTION MODE

DAY-10

Daily Journaling (morning)

Gratitude Letter

Habit 1-

Drink Water-   (Hot Water *with* Lemon)

(Hot Water with cumin & saunf)

Exercise-   Yes/No

Duration-

Feeling After Exercise-

Works to be done today-   Done/Not done

Work 1

Work 2

Work 3

Work 4

Work 5

Night Routine

How was your Day-

What are the things you achieved

What you are thankful of-

ACTION MODE

DAY-11

Daily Journaling (morning)

Gratitude Letter

Habit 1-

Drink Water-   (Hot Water *with* Lemon)

          (Hot Water with cumin & saunf)

Exercise-   Yes/No

Duration-

Feeling After Exercise-

Works to be done today-   Done/Not done

Work 1

Work 2

Work 3

Work 4

Work 5

Night Routine

How was your Day-

What are the things you achieved

What you are thankful of-

ACTION MODE

DAY-12

Daily Journaling (morning)

Gratitude Letter

Habit 1-

Drink Water-   (Hot Water *with* Lemon)

          (Hot Water with cumin & saunf)

Exercise-   Yes/No

Duration-

Feeling After Exercise-

Works to be done today-   Done/Not done

Work 1

Work 2

Work 3

Work 4

Work 5

Night Routine

How was your Day-

What are the things you achieved

What you are thankful of-

ACTION MODE

DAY-13

Daily Journaling (morning)

Gratitude Letter

Habit 1-

Drink Water-   (Hot Water *with* Lemon)

                 (Hot Water with cumin & saunf)

Exercise-   Yes/No

Duration-

Feeling After Exercise-

Works to be done today-   Done/Not done

Work 1

Work 2

Work 3

Work 4

Work 5

Night Routine

How was your Day-

What are the things you achieved

What you are thankful of-

ACTION MODE

DAY-14

Daily Journaling (morning)

Gratitude Letter

Habit 1-

Drink Water- (Hot Water *with* Lemon)

(Hot Water with cumin & saunf)

Exercise- Yes/No

Duration-

Feeling After Exercise-

Works to be done today- Done/Not done

Work 1

Work 2

Work 3

Work 4

Work 5

Night Routine

How was your Day-

What are the things you achieved

What you are thankful of-

ACTION MODE

DAY-15

Daily Journaling (morning)

Gratitude Letter

Habit 1-

Drink Water-　　(Hot Water *with* Lemon)

　　　　　　　　(Hot Water with cumin & saunf)

Exercise-　　　　Yes/No

Duration-

Feeling After Exercise-

Works to be done today-　　Done/Not done

Work 1

Work 2

Work 3

Work 4

Work 5

Night Routine

How was your Day-

What are the things you achieved

What you are thankful of-

ACTION MODE

DAY-16

Daily Journaling (morning)

Gratitude Letter

Habit 1-

Drink Water-   (Hot Water *with* Lemon)

                (Hot Water with cumin & saunf)

Exercise-   Yes/No

Duration-

Feeling After Exercise-

Works to be done today-   Done/Not done

Work 1

Work 2

Work 3

Work 4

Work 5

Night Routine

How was your Day-

What are the things you achieved

What you are thankful of-

ACTION MODE

DAY-17

Daily Journaling (morning)

Gratitude Letter

Habit 1-

Drink Water-   (Hot Water *with* Lemon)

   (Hot Water with cumin & saunf)

Exercise-   Yes/No

Duration-

Feeling After Exercise-

Works to be done today-   Done/Not done

Work 1

Work 2

Work 3

Work 4

Work 5

Night Routine

How was your Day-

What are the things you achieved

What you are thankful of-

ACTION MODE

DAY-18

Daily Journaling (morning)

Gratitude Letter

Habit 1-

Drink Water-   (Hot Water *with* Lemon)

(Hot Water with cumin & saunf)

Exercise-   Yes/No

Duration-

Feeling After Exercise-

Works to be done today-   Done/Not done

Work 1

Work 2

Work 3

Work 4

Work 5

Night Routine

How was your Day-

What are the things you achieved

What you are thankful of-

ACTION MODE

DAY-19

Daily Journaling (morning)

Gratitude Letter

Habit 1-

Drink Water-   (Hot Water *with* Lemon)

              (Hot Water with cumin & saunf)

Exercise-   Yes/No

Duration-

Feeling After Exercise-

Works to be done today-   Done/Not done

Work 1

Work 2

Work 3

Work 4

Work 5

Night Routine

How was your Day-

What are the things you achieved

What you are thankful of-

ACTION MODE

DAY-20

Daily Journaling (morning)

Gratitude Letter

Habit 1-

Drink Water-   (Hot Water *with* Lemon)

　　　　　　　(Hot Water with cumin & saunf)

Exercise-   Yes/No

Duration-

Feeling After Exercise-

Works to be done today-   Done/Not done

Work 1

Work 2

Work 3

Work 4

Work 5

Night Routine

How was your Day-

What are the things you achieved

What you are thankful of-

ACTION MODE

DAY-21

Daily Journaling (morning)

Gratitude Letter

Habit 1-

Drink Water-   (Hot Water *with* Lemon)

(Hot Water with cumin & saunf)

Exercise-   Yes/No

Duration-

Feeling After Exercise-

Works to be done today-   Done/Not done

Work 1

Work 2

Work 3

Work 4

Work 5

Night Routine

How was your Day-

What are the things you achieved

What you are thankful of-

ACTION MODE

DAY-22

Daily Journaling (morning)

Gratitude Letter

Habit 1-

Drink Water-   (Hot Water *with* Lemon)

(Hot Water with cumin & saunf)

Exercise-   Yes/No

Duration-

Feeling After Exercise-

Works to be done today-   Done/Not done

Work 1

Work 2

Work 3

Work 4

Work 5

Night Routine

How was your Day-

What are the things you achieved

What you are thankful of-

ACTION MODE

DAY-23

Daily Journaling (morning)

Gratitude Letter

Habit 1-

Drink Water-   (Hot Water *with* Lemon)

                              (Hot Water with cumin & saunf)

Exercise-   Yes/No

Duration-

Feeling After Exercise-

Works to be done today-   Done/Not done

Work 1

Work 2

Work 3

Work 4

Work 5

Night Routine

How was your Day-

What are the things you achieved

What you are thankful of-

ACTION MODE

DAY-24

Daily Journaling (morning)

Gratitude Letter

Habit 1-

Drink Water-   (Hot Water *with* Lemon)

(Hot Water with cumin & saunf)

Exercise-   Yes/No

Duration-

Feeling After Exercise-

Works to be done today-   Done/Not done

Work 1

Work 2

Work 3

Work 4

Work 5

Night Routine

How was your Day-

What are the things you achieved

What you are thankful of-

ACTION MODE

DAY-25

Daily Journaling (morning)

Gratitude Letter

Habit 1-

Drink Water-   (Hot Water *with* Lemon)

              (Hot Water with cumin & saunf)

Exercise-   Yes/No

Duration-

Feeling After Exercise-

Works to be done today-   Done/Not done

Work 1

Work 2

Work 3

Work 4

Work 5

Night Routine

How was your Day-

What are the things you achieved

What you are thankful of-

ACTION MODE

DAY-26

Daily Journaling (morning)

Gratitude Letter

Habit 1-

Drink Water-   (Hot Water *with* Lemon)

(Hot Water with cumin & saunf)

Exercise-   Yes/No

Duration-

Feeling After Exercise-

Works to be done today-   Done/Not done

Work 1

Work 2

Work 3

Work 4

Work 5

Night Routine

How was your Day-

What are the things you achieved

What you are thankful of-

ACTION MODE

DAY-27

Daily Journaling (morning)

Gratitude Letter

Habit 1-

Drink Water-   (Hot Water *with* Lemon)

(Hot Water with cumin & saunf)

Exercise-   Yes/No

Duration-

Feeling After Exercise-

Works to be done today-   Done/Not done

Work 1

Work 2

Work 3

Work 4

Work 5

Night Routine

How was your Day-

What are the things you achieved

What you are thankful of-

ACTION MODE

DAY-28

Daily Journaling (morning)

Gratitude Letter

Habit 1-

Drink Water-   (Hot Water *with* Lemon)

   (Hot Water with cumin & saunf)

Exercise-   Yes/No

Duration-

Feeling After Exercise-

Works to be done today-   Done/Not done

Work 1

Work 2

Work 3

Work 4

Work 5

Night Routine

How was your Day-

What are the things you achieved

What you are thankful of-

ACTION MODE

DAY-29

Daily Journaling (morning)

Gratitude Letter

Habit 1-

Drink Water-   (Hot Water *with* Lemon)

                 (Hot Water with cumin & saunf)

Exercise-   Yes/No

Duration-

Feeling After Exercise-

Works to be done today-   Done/Not done

Work 1

Work 2

Work 3

Work 4

Work 5

Night Routine

How was your Day-

What are the things you achieved

What you are thankful of-

ACTION MODE

DAY-30

Daily Journaling (morning)

Gratitude Letter

Habit 1-

Drink Water-   (Hot Water *with* Lemon)

                    (Hot Water with cumin & saunf)

Exercise-   Yes/No

Duration-

Feeling After Exercise-

Works to be done today-   Done/Not done

Work 1

Work 2

Work 3

Work 4

Work 5

Night Routine

How was your Day-

What are the things you achieved

What you are thankful of-

Timelessness-Experience your life after 1 year

Letter to your dear self

Dear ....

MY SMAAC GOALS

- **S** — Specific
- **M** — Measureble
- **A** —
- **A** — Achievable
- **C** — Commitable

MY GOALS

1. Personal Goals

1-

2-

3-

4-

5-

Action Steps

_____

_____

_____

2. Health Goals

1-

2-

3-

4-

5-

Action Steps

_____

_____

_____

_____

3. Relationships Goals

1-

2-

3-

4-

5-

Action Steps

_____

_____

_____

_____

4. Financial Goals

1-

2-

3-

4-

5-

Action Steps

_____

_____

_____

_____

5. Fun and Leisure Goals

1-

2-

3-

4-

5-

Action Steps

_____

_____

_____

_____

MY HAPPY CORNER

BEAUTIFUL MOMENTS
_____
_____
_____

SPARK MOMENTS
(Moments of Quality time with family)
_____
_____
_____

SELF-LOVE MOMENTS
_____
_____
_____

GRATITUDE

KHUSHI KA DABBA

(HAPPY

LETS DRAW AND ADD COLOUR TO YOUR GOALS

Affirmation

Accept your feelings

Feeling Rejected

Feeling Frustrated

Burning Bowl

Write Feelings bother you

Tear it

Burn It

Repeat let go while looking to flame

Acts of kindness

Switch Game- Pivot it

NEGATIVE THOUGHT (OLD)	SWITCH IT (NEW THOUGHTS)

Let go Practice

What do you want to let go?

_____

_____

_____

_____

_____

Let go mediation
link-
https://youtu.be/YZQuCVOMduw?si=ZxUVQu0QUVgzvnGU
Anatomy & life transformation talks.
Subscribe, Like & share

ENERGY ZAPPERS

100% BATTERY

LOW BATTERY

_____

_____

_____

_____

_____

_____

_____

_____

ENERGY BOOSTERS

_____
_____
_____
_____
_____
_____
_____

SPARK TEAM

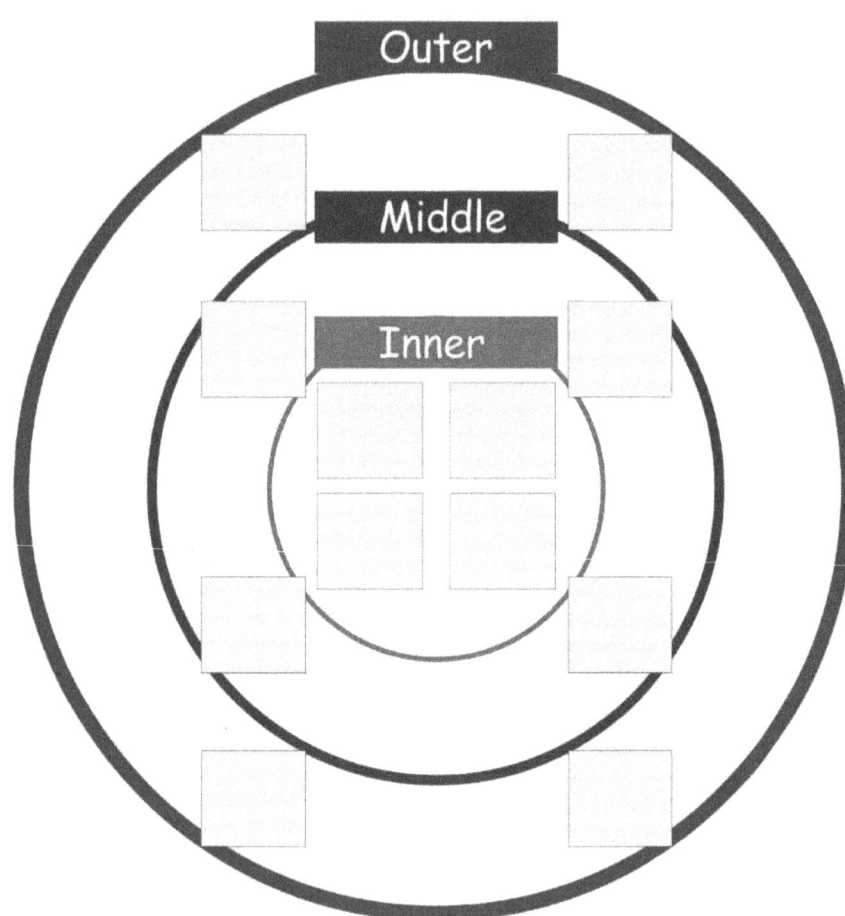

* Put name of person in each circle or boxes.

AMAZING HABITS YOU HAVE

1- Habit 1   ex- As soon I get up.

Tag one habit you want to do.........?
Eg. Drink warm water.

2- Habit -2

Tag Habit -2

_____

_____

_____

3- Habit - 3

Tag Habit-3

_____

_____

_____

4- Habit – 4

Tag habit – 4

_____

_____

_____

5- Habit 5

Tag habit 5

_____

_____

_____

6- Habit 6

Tag habit 6

_____

_____

_____

7- Habit 7

Tag habit 7

_____

_____

_____

8- Habit 8

Tag habit 8

_____

_____

_____

9- Habit 9

Tag Habit 9

_____

_____

_____

10- Habit 10

Tag Habit

_____

_____

_____

Negative Self Beliefs

How to improve?	
What you want to believe?	
Is this universal truth?	

From where did I pick that from?

About myself

Best Childhood Memories

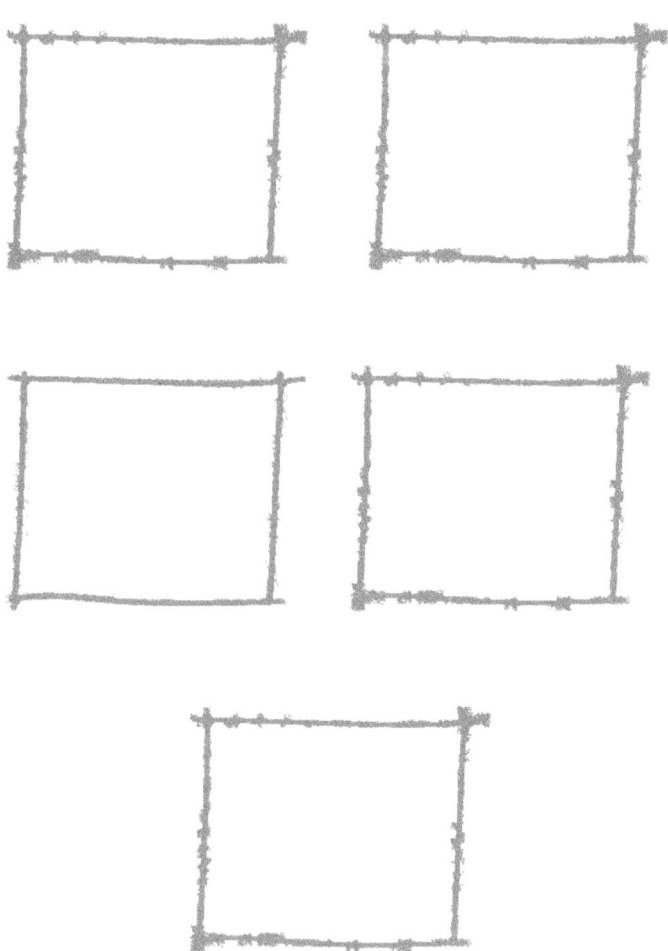

Worst Childhood Memories

Moments you feel rejected

Free Links- Youtube channel Anatomy and life transformation talks

https://www.youtube.com/@anatomymadeeasyclassesby dr5583

New Empowering Habit

LET'S TALK MONEY

Love letter to money

ARIGATO MONEY

(THANK YOU MONEY)

When you receive	When you give
I appreciate the flow of financial blessings in my life	I appreciate the large amount of money coming to me so that I am able to pay my bills easily

ARIGATO MONEY PRACTICE TRACKER

(Put a tick (✓) when done)

WEEK 1	WEEK 2	WEEK 3	WEEK 4
DAY 1	DAY 1	DAY 1	DAY 1
DAY 2	DAY 2	DAY 2	DAY 2
DAY 3	DAY 3	DAY 3	DAY 3

DAY 4	DAY 4	DAY 4	DAY 4
DAY 5	DAY 5	DAY 5	DAY 5
DAY 6	DAY 6	DAY 6	DAY 6
DAY 7	DAY 7	DAY 7	DAY 7

ARIGATO MONEY PRACTICE TRACKER

(Put a tick (✓) when done)

WEEK 1	WEEK 2	WEEK 3	WEEK 4
DAY 1	DAY 1	DAY 1	DAY 1
DAY 2	DAY 2	DAY 2	DAY 2
DAY 3	DAY 3	DAY 3	DAY 3

DAY 4	DAY 4	DAY 4	DAY 4
DAY 5	DAY 5	DAY 5	DAY 5
DAY 6	DAY 6	DAY 6	DAY 6
DAY 7	DAY 7	DAY 7	DAY 7

ARIGATO MONEY PRACTICE TRACKER

(Put a tick (✓) when done)

WEEK 1	WEEK 2	WEEK 3	WEEK 4
DAY 1	DAY 1	DAY 1	DAY 1
DAY 2	DAY 2	DAY 2	DAY 2
DAY 3	DAY 3	DAY 3	DAY 3

DAY 4	DAY 4	DAY 4	DAY 4
DAY 5	DAY 5	DAY 5	DAY 5
DAY 6	DAY 6	DAY 6	DAY 6
DAY 7	DAY 7	DAY 7	DAY 7

ARIGATO MONEY PRACTICE TRACKER

(Put a tick (✓) when done)

WEEK 1	WEEK 2	WEEK 3	WEEK 4
DAY 1	DAY 1	DAY 1	DAY 1
DAY 2	DAY 2	DAY 2	DAY 2
DAY 3	DAY 3	DAY 3	DAY 3

DAY 4	DAY 4	DAY 4	DAY 4
DAY 5	DAY 5	DAY 5	DAY 5
DAY 6	DAY 6	DAY 6	DAY 6
DAY 7	DAY 7	DAY 7	DAY 7

ARIGATO MONEY PRACTICE TRACKER

(Put a tick (✓) when done)

WEEK 1	WEEK 2	WEEK 3	WEEK 4
DAY 1	DAY 1	DAY 1	DAY 1
DAY 2	DAY 2	DAY 2	DAY 2
DAY 3	DAY 3	DAY 3	DAY 3

DAY 4	DAY 4	DAY 4	DAY 4
DAY 5	DAY 5	DAY 5	DAY 5
DAY 6	DAY 6	DAY 6	DAY 6
DAY 7	DAY 7	DAY 7	DAY 7

My Happy Corner

BEAUTIFUL MOMENTS

THANKFUL MOMENTS

GRATITUDE MOMENTS

TOP 3 GOALS FOR THIS YEAR

GOAL 1

GOAL 2

GOAL 3

GOAL 1

Challenges _____

_____

_____

_____

_____

_____

Empowering Steps

_____

_____

_____

_____

_____

GOAL 2

Challenges _____
_____
_____
_____
_____
_____

Empowering Steps

_____
_____
_____
_____
_____

GOAL 3

Challenges _____

_____

_____

_____

_____

Empowering Steps

_____

_____

_____

_____

_____

Moments

WHEN YOU OVERCOME FEAR

_____
_____
_____
_____
_____
_____
_____
_____
_____
_____
_____
_____
_____
_____
_____
_____
_____

ART THERAPY

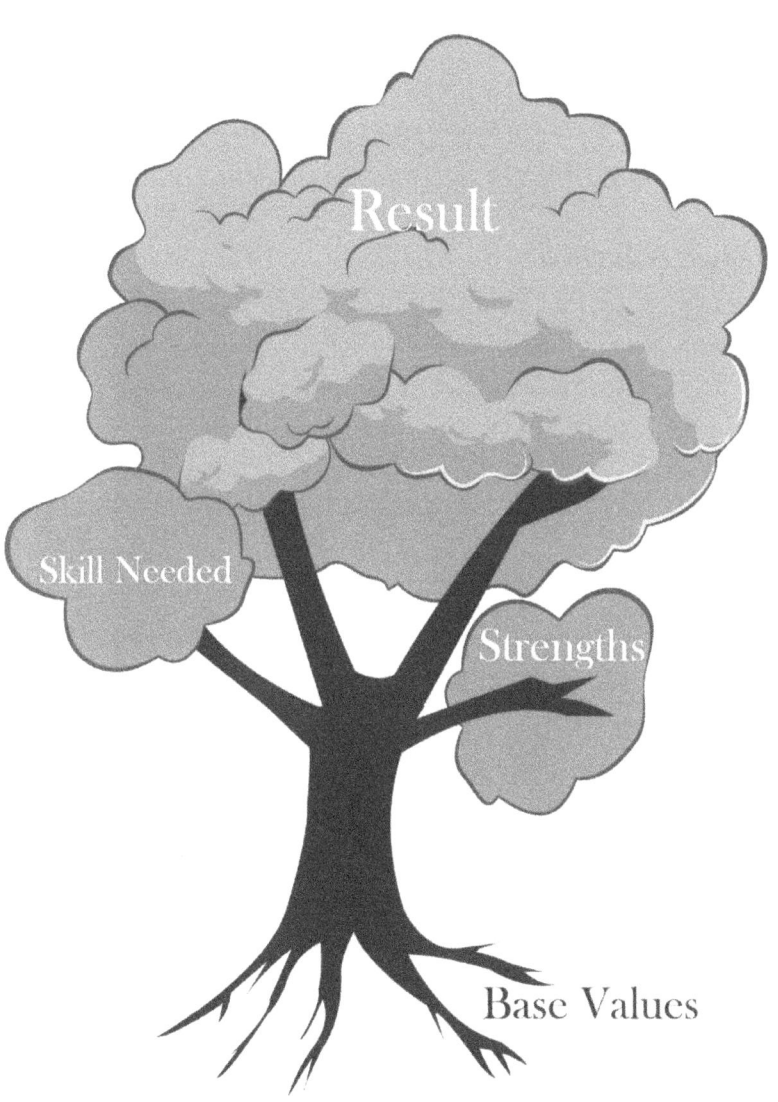

PROGRESS CHART

Result Achieved

        New Skills Acquired

                Consistent Habbits

                      New habbits acquired

NEW HABBITS ACQUIRED

_____
_____
_____
_____
_____
_____
_____
_____
_____
_____
_____
_____
_____
_____
_____
_____

Books Recommendation

- ✓ Atomic Habits – James Clear
- ✓ The every day Hero Manifesto – Robin Sharma
- ✓ Zero limits – Joe Vitale

Make your own book list

_____

_____

_____

_____

_____

_____

_____

_____

_____

Reading Club

Name of book you are reading

_____
_____
_____
_____
_____
_____
_____
_____
_____
_____
_____
_____

LEARNING OF THE BOOK

DAY 1

Day 2

Day 3

Day 4

Day 5

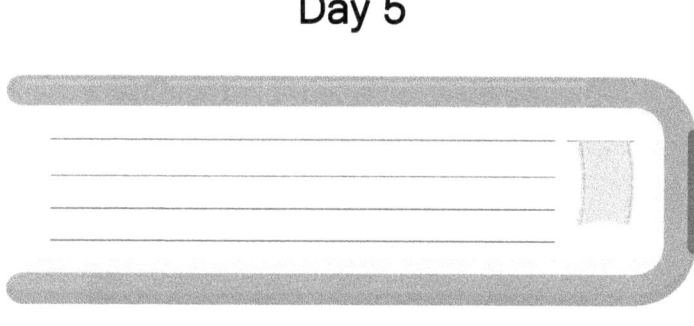

Day 6

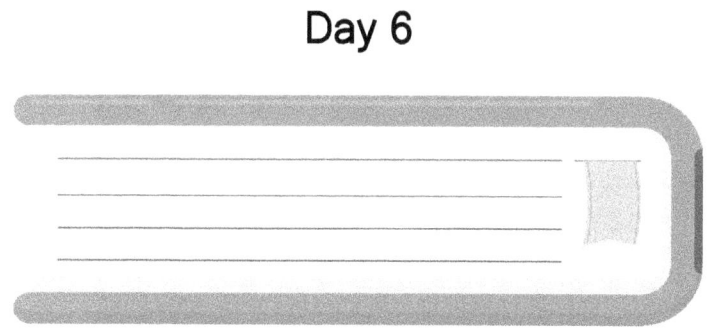

Day 7

Day 8

Day 9

Day 10

Day 11

Day 12

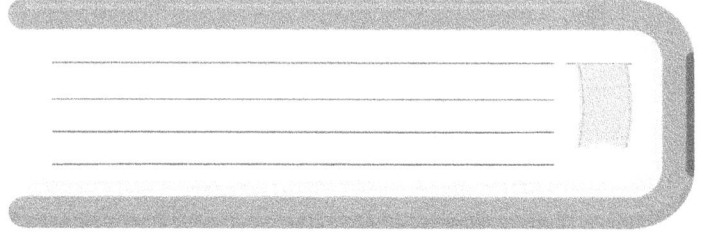

Day 13

Day 14

Day 15

Day 16

Day 17

Day 18

Day 19

Day 20

Day 21

Day 22

Day 23

Day 24

Day 25

Day 26

Day 27

Day 28

Day 29

Day 30

PIVOTING

Switch your negative thoughts with positive ones.

OLD THOUGHT	NEW THOUGHT

OLD THOUGHT	NEW THOUGHT

OLD THOUGHT	NEW THOUGHT

OLD THOUGHT	NEW THOUGHT

Things you admire about yourself.

_____

_____

_____

_____

_____

_____

_____

_____

_____

_____

_____

_____

_____

Things which you do not like about yourself.

GOALS WHICH YOU ACHIEVED AFTER 1 YEAR.

HEALTH GOALS

WEALTH GOALS

FUN & LEISURE

RELATIONSHIP

CAREER

LIST OF PEOPLE WITH WHOM YOU LIKE TO SPEND TIME

GIVE THEM RATING FROM 0 TO 10

01 _____

02 _____

03 _____

04 _____

05 _____

06 _____

07 _____

08 _____

09 _____

10 _____

MY VISION BOARD

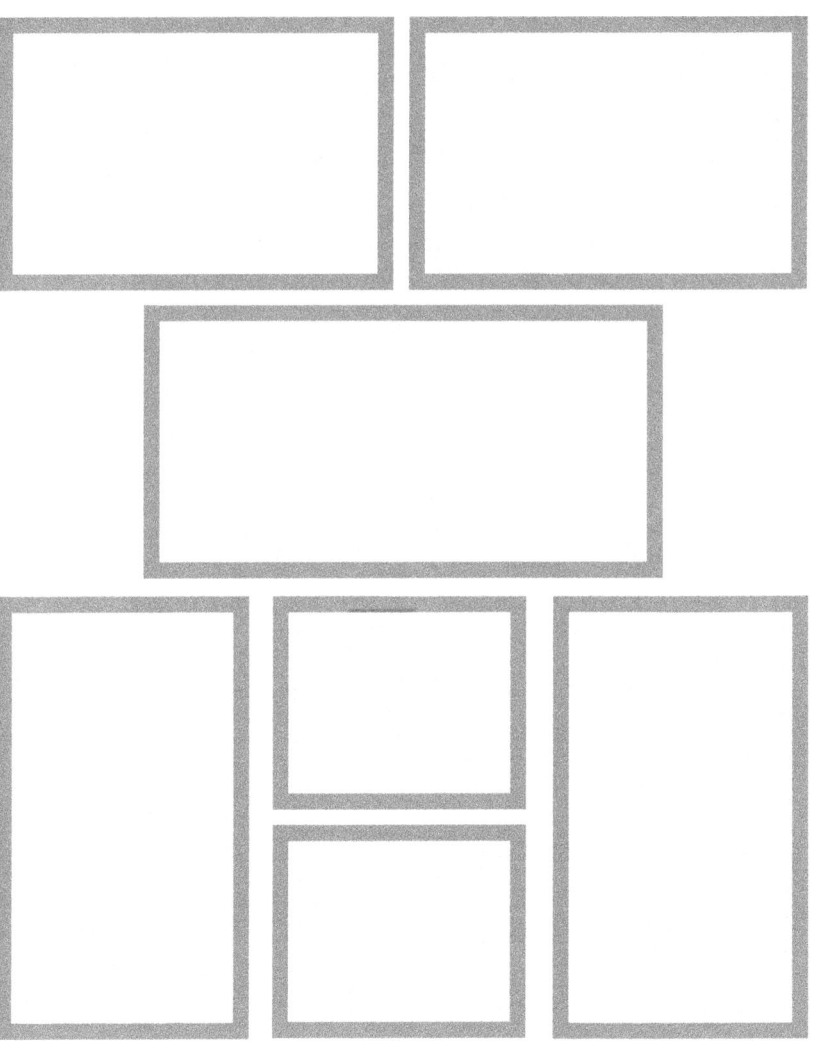

BLOCKS IN YOUR SUCCESS

STEPS TO REMOVE THIS

MY CRAZY COURAGEOUS DREAMS

_____
_____
_____
_____
_____
_____
_____
_____
_____
_____
_____
_____

HAPPINESS METER

DAY-1
How you are feeling

Morning

_____
_____
_____
_____

Afternoon

_____
_____
_____
_____

Night

_____
_____
_____
_____

HAPPINESS METER

DAY-2

How you are feeling

Morning

_____
_____
_____
_____

Afternoon

_____
_____
_____
_____

Night

_____
_____
_____
_____

HAPPINESS METER

DAY-3

How you are feeling

Morning

_____
_____
_____
_____

Afternoon

_____
_____
_____
_____

Night

_____
_____
_____
_____

HAPPINESS METER

DAY-4

How you are feeling

Morning

_____
_____
_____
_____

Afternoon

_____
_____
_____
_____

Night

_____
_____
_____
_____

HAPPINESS METER

DAY-5
How you are feeling

Morning

_____
_____
_____
_____

Afternoon

_____
_____
_____
_____

Night

_____
_____
_____
_____

HAPPINESS METER

DAY-6

How you are feeling

Morning

_____
_____
_____
_____

Afternoon

_____
_____
_____
_____

Night

_____
_____
_____
_____

HAPPINESS METER

DAY-7
How you are feeling

Morning

_____
_____
_____
_____

Afternoon

_____
_____
_____
_____

Night

_____
_____
_____
_____

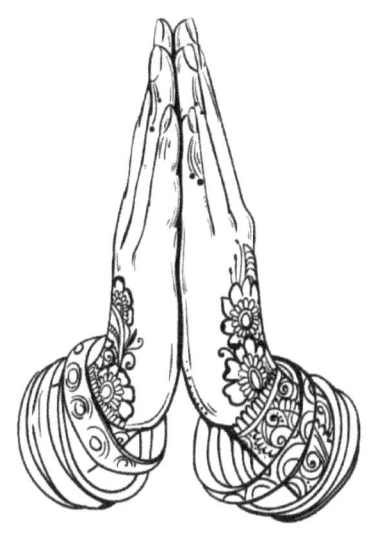

Power of Prayer

Let's cleanse with

HOPONOPONO

(ancient Hawaiian prayer).

I love you .
I am sorry
Please forgive me.
I let go.

Apply this to people, things and situation.

_____

_____

_____

_____

_____

_____

_____

_____

_____

_____

_____

_____

_____

For details.

Contact -your life coach and healer.

Dr Amrita Kumari.

You tube link.
https://youtu.be/cqypf9gWB28?si=bBiA9TwW5LPxB3yO

MOMENTS WHEN YOU ARE JUDGED

MOMENTS WHEN YOU JUDGED SOMEONE

_____
_____
_____
_____
_____
_____
_____
_____
_____
_____
_____
_____
_____
_____
_____

REGRETS OF YOUR LIFE

_____
_____
_____
_____
_____
_____
_____
_____
_____
_____
_____
_____
_____
_____
_____
_____

THINGS YOU WANT TO LET GO

SAD MOMENTS OF YOUR LIFE

Happiest moments of your life

_____
_____
_____
_____
_____
_____
_____
_____

Cheerful Memories

INTENTION

FOR WEEK

WEEK 1 Work to be done.	Why you need to do the work?	How do you feel after doing the work
(Day 1)		
Day 2		
Day 3		
Day 4		
Day 5		
Day 6		
Day 7		

INTENTION
FOR WEEK

WEEK 2 Work to be done.	Why you need to do the work?	How do you feel after doing the work
(Day 1)		
Day 2		
Day 3		
Day 4		
Day 5		
Day 6		
Day 7		

INTENTION
FOR WEEK

WEEK 3 Work to be done.	Why you need to do the work?	How do you feel after doing the work
(Day 1)		
Day 2		
Day 3		
Day 4		
Day 5		
Day 6		
Day 7		

INTENTION
FOR WEEK

WEEK 4 Work to be done.	Why you need to do the work?	How do you feel after doing the work
(Day 1)		
Day 2		
Day 3		
Day 4		
Day 5		
Day 6		
Day 7		

INTENTION
FOR WEEK

WEEK 5 Work to be done.	Why you need to do the work?	How do you feel after doing the work
(Day 1)		
Day 2		
Day 3		
Day 4		
Day 5		
Day 6		
Day 7		

INTENTION
FOR WEEK

WEEK 6 Work to be done.	Why you need to do the work?	How do you feel after doing the work
(Day 1)		
Day 2		
Day 3		
Day 4		
Day 5		
Day 6		
Day 7		

INTENTION
FOR WEEK

WEEK 7 Work to be done.	Why you need to do the work?	How do you feel after doing the work
(Day 1)		
Day 2		
Day 3		
Day 4		
Day 5		
Day 6		
Day 7		

INTENTION OF DAY-1

Work to be done

Why it is needed

How you feel after that

INTENTION OF DAY-2

Work to be done	Why it is needed	How you feel after that

INTENTION OF DAY-3

Work to be done	Why it is needed	How you feel after that

INTENTION OF DAY-4

Work to be done	Why it is needed	How you feel after that

INTENTION OF DAY-5

Work to be done	Why it is needed	How you feel after that

INTENTION OF DAY-6

Work to be done	Why it is needed	How you feel after that

INTENTION OF DAY-7

Work to be done	Why it is needed	How you feel after that

INTENTION OF DAY-8

Work to be done	Why it is needed	How you feel after that

INTENTION OF DAY-9

Work to be done	Why it is needed	How you feel after that

INTENTION OF DAY-10

Work to be done	Why it is needed	How you feel after that

INTENTION OF DAY-11

Work to be done	Why it is needed	How you feel after that

INTENTION OF DAY-12

Work to be done	Why it is needed	How you feel after that

INTENTION OF DAY-13

Work to be done	Why it is needed	How you feel after that

INTENTION OF DAY-14

Work to be done	Why it is needed	How you feel after that

INTENTION OF DAY-15

Work to be done	Why it is needed	How you feel after that

INTENTION OF DAY-16

Work to be done	Why it is needed	How you feel after that

INTENTION OF DAY-17

Work to be done	Why it is needed	How you feel after that

INTENTION OF DAY-18

Work to be done	Why it is needed	How you feel after that

INTENTION OF DAY-19

Work to be done

Why it is needed

How you feel after that

INTENTION OF DAY-20

Work to be done

Why it is needed

How you feel after that

INTENTION OF DAY-21

Work to be done	Why it is needed	How you feel after that

INTENTION OF DAY-22

Work to be done	Why it is needed	How you feel after that

INTENTION OF DAY-23

Work to be done	Why it is needed	How you feel after that

INTENTION OF DAY-24

Work to be done	Why it is needed	How you feel after that

INTENTION OF DAY-25

Work to be done	Why it is needed	How you feel after that

INTENTION OF DAY-26

Work to be done	Why it is needed	How you feel after that

INTENTION OF DAY-27

Work to be done	Why it is needed	How you feel after that

INTENTION OF DAY-28

Work to be done	Why it is needed	How you feel after that

INTENTION OF DAY-29

Work to be done	Why it is needed	How you feel after that

INTENTION OF DAY-30

Work to be done	Why it is needed	How you feel after that

INTENTION OF DAY-31

Work to be done	Why it is needed	How you feel after that

Moments which made you a better person

Person to whom you feel grateful

_____
_____
_____
_____
_____
_____
_____
_____
_____
_____
_____
_____
_____

Moments of Gratitude

Moments of Happiness

What is your progress with this journal?

MY FUTURE SELF

WHEEL OF LIFE

WHERE I AM

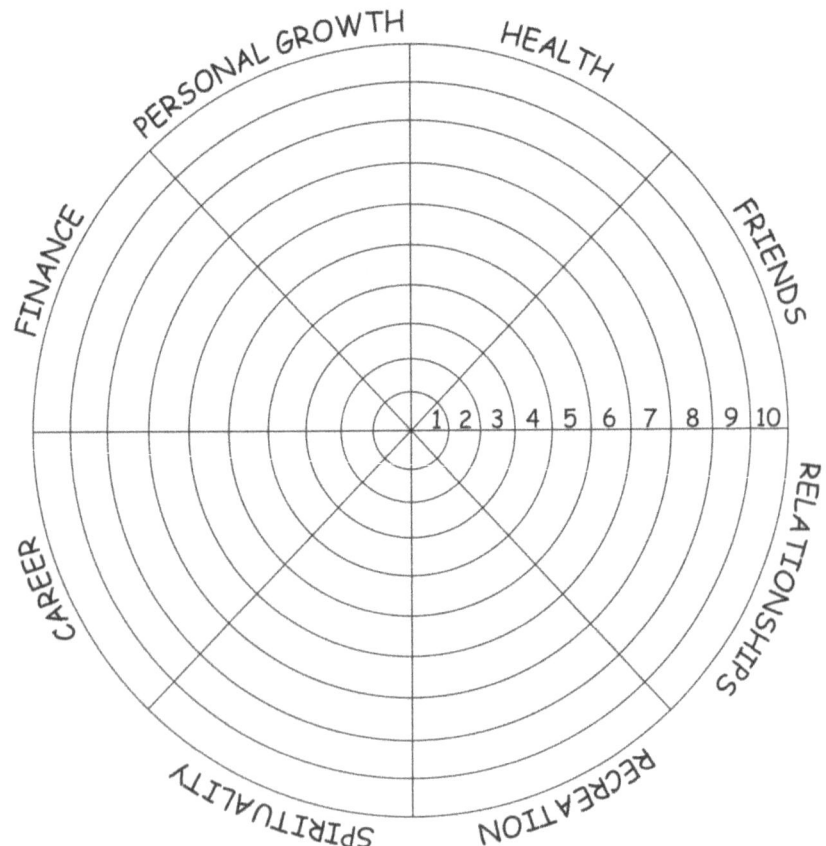

www.ingramcontent.com/pod-product-compliance
Lightning Source LLC
LaVergne TN
LVHW061543070526
838199LV00077B/6888